Until the day his arms turned white—
Like polar bears on ice.
His heart sank low—a scary sight—
For leprosy's *not nice*!

Poor Naaman thought his days were few;
He bowed his head and cried.
He didn't know what they would do
If suddenly, he died.

Now Naaman knew a young girl who
Did serve his wife each day.
The young girl said, "Please listen to
All that I have to say.

"My God is strong, and He can do
Some pretty nifty stuff.
And He has sent a prophet who
Has faith that's strong enough.

"Samaria's the place to go
To find this holy man.
My master has such pain and woe—
Go find him, if you can."

So Naaman asked his boss, the king,
If he could take a break.
The king said, "Yes, and with you bring
An offer that I'll make."

The king of Aram sent him where
He hoped he could persuade
The king of Israel to dare
To come to Naaman's aid.

But that old king was overwrought—
"I can't cure leprosy!"
He feared a fight was what was sought—
"O woe, O woe is me!"

Elisha heard of the king's woes
And said, "God will provide
A miracle so Naaman knows
God's love is deep and wide."

Elisha said, "Go dip into
The Jordan's cleansing tide.
For seven baths will restore you—
You'll have a brand-new hide."

Elisha's words sparked Naaman's wrath,
But his friends set him straight.
When Naaman took that holy bath,
It washed away his rage.

For on that day the soldier's skin
Was new like a young boy's.
And God forgave him of his sin;
His heart was filled with joy.

Through the muddy waters of Jordan,
God a healing did provide.
And in the waters of Baptism,
God's grace and life abide.

Dear Parents,

This Bible story can be used to teach children about God's love, grace, and forgiveness. God used the muddy waters of Jordan to heal the disease that ravaged Naaman's body. Unlikely? Yes, but part of God's plan. He used a baby born in a stable to bring healing for the sin that ravages each of *us*. Unlikely? Yes, but part of God's plan for our salvation. And through the waters of Baptism, God washes away the eternal punishment of our sin as He makes us His very own. He makes it possible for us to share in the life, death, and resurrection of His Son, our Savior.

Talk with your child about sin—those things we do wrong that separate us from God. Make a list of sins—as many as can fit on one sheet of paper. Then use lemon juice to draw a large cross on the paper, from top to bottom, and side to side. The cross will appear as you hold the paper over a bare light bulb. (Be sure not to hold the paper too close!)

Remember each day the healing God has brought to all of us through Jesus' cross. Live in the light of His forgiveness and share this good news with others.

The Editor